"If one were contemplating throwing in the towel or were found in a state of lost hope due to life's endless challenges, then this Holy Spirit led piece of writing by Lisa Rufaro will change your course and re-ignite your faith. I encourage you to follow this faith moving account on how very young, humble Lisa and her family, through prayer and unwavering trust in God prevailed over some of the most unimaginable battles in life."

—*[Blessing T. Kavai -*
Intercessor, Prayer Counselor
and Lay Preacher....also
Aviation Safety Practitioner]

Here I Am:

Tears

of an African Immigrant

Book 1: Family Values

LISA RUFARO

WESTBOW
PRESS®
A DIVISION OF THOMAS NELSON
& ZONDERVAN

Scriptures taken from the Holy Bible, New International Version®,
NIV®. Copyright © 1973, 1978, 1984, 2011 by Biblica, Inc.™ Used
by permission of Zondervan. All rights reserved worldwide. www.
zondervan.com <http://www.zondervan.com/> The "NIV" and
"New International Version" are trademarks registered in the
United States Patent and Trademark Office by Biblica, Inc.™

This book is a work of non-fiction. Unless otherwise
noted, the author and the publisher make no explicit
guarantees as to the accuracy of the information contained
in this book and in some cases, names of people and
places have been altered to protect their privacy.

WestBow Press books may be ordered through
booksellers or by contacting:

WestBow Press
A Division of Thomas Nelson & Zondervan
1663 Liberty Drive
Bloomington, IN 47403
www.westbowpress.com
1 (866) 928-1240

Because of the dynamic nature of the Internet, any web
addresses or links contained in this book may have changed
since publication and may no longer be valid. The views
expressed in this work are solely those of the author and do
not necessarily reflect the views of the publisher, and the
publisher hereby disclaims any responsibility for them.

Any people depicted in stock imagery provided
by Thinkstock are models, and such images are
being used for illustrative purposes only.
Certain stock imagery © Thinkstock.

ISBN: 978-1-5127-9700-8 (sc)
ISBN: 978-1-5127-9701-5 (e)

Library of Congress Control Number: 2017911555

Print information available on the last page.

WestBow Press rev. date: 08/03/2017

CONTENTS

PREFACE

This book is an episodic memoir. All the chapters highlight true stories as well as individual themes. I incorporated others' memories to provide further details about events that took place primarily in my childhood.

The purpose of this book is to provide my perspective on how past events occurred to my family, how I reacted to them, and how they contributed to my faith as a born-again believer in Jesus Christ. I want my story to prompt others to practice self-reflection and authenticity before God through life's challenges.

We all desperately need God and can make it through unimaginable trials only with His strength when we are weak.

This book will challenge readers to persevere in prayer during difficult times, know there is a purpose for every tribulation they experience, and glorify God with their testimony. *Family Values* is the first book in the series, "Here I Am: Tears of an African Immigrant."

To present clear and concise chapters, some timelines were abridged. Nicknames and Shona terms from Zimbabwe are italicized with English translation with some names modified.

ACKNOWLEDGMENTS

I have gone through an invigorating and challenging season in my life that stretched my faith in God to new heights. This note of thanks comes with much joy. I have learned so much about myself by discovering abilities that were in me from before I was born and seeing a new side of God. So often, we do not know what we are capable of, and I give all honor and glory to my Lord and Savior Jesus Christ.

I reflect here on the people who have supported and helped me so much throughout this period.

A sincere thank you to my parents and my mother in particular. Thank you for instilling the fear of God in me and always encouraging me. Thank you to my older brother; your life has impacted me in more ways than you understand and will continue to touch many people for God's glory.

I also thank the family of God I have had the privilege to serve alongside.

Thank you with agape love!

CHAPTER 1

I Always Knew God Was Real

A lot happened in 1998. At the time, I did not fully comprehend the dynamics of what my parents were sacrificing for our family to relocate to the United States. I was seven when the plans began to materialize. Zimbabwe's economic condition in general and discord in my paternal family in particular had pledged allegiance to each other, and this was the reason for our migration. But more than anything else, paternal family conflicts seemed to be the leader of the coalition. All my life, I knew there were various tensions in the paternal clan, but it was still difficult to pinpoint what they were. They must have stemmed from jealousy, envy, and insecurities. Despite the

1

source, I have always been thankful to God for my life and for my resilient parents.

I do not think I ever told my parents that even when I was just four, I always told myself in a light, soft voice that I felt God told me everything would be all right. I would close my eyes, knowing God was watching me in a comforting manner, and I would repeat, "Everything is going to be all right."

As a child, I was exposed to many things children typically do not fully comprehend until adulthood if ever. I always knew God was real; nobody had to convince me of that. If anything, my parents instilled the fear of God in me, but it was as if I had already recognized the Holy Spirit's comforting presence.

My parents have always been able to withstand and recover quickly from difficult situations. Most of the difficult seasons they experienced seemed always to stem from some members of our extended family. Family strife on my father's side played a huge role in forming the woman I have become today. I am thankful for my parents. It would all make more sense later as an adult when I learned of the story of Joseph in the Bible; there are clear parallels. After experiencing such betrayal by your blood, what would all the midnight tears amount to? Struggles and pain experienced in a foreign country. Feelings of lost roots and no family support. Divine insights gained through the interpretation of dreams and visions. Battles against the Egyptians in our lives—the coalition as I referred to them. Despite Pharaoh's pursuit, realizing all the trials were for our family's sanctification—being set apart for such a time as this.

There I was, an African immigrant in tears. I often think of Genesis 50:20 (NIV): "You intended to harm me, but God intended it for good to accomplish what is now being done, the saving of many lives."

I am thankful for my parents and for my resilient, prayer-warrior mother in particular. They taught me to pursue God and to work hard to achieve my aspirations.

Like Joseph, my parents had a lot of things going their way in life at first. They had successful careers. So many times, I observed their generosity to extended family for housing and education expenses. They were raising beautiful children in their happy home, which was designed and built from scratch—and was therefore a target of the enemy.

While my father and mother had great dreams that made them feel good about themselves, one day, our lives changed. Can you imagine how it must have felt to know a few paternal family members despised you so much that they would resort to unholy divination and schemes just to have their way?

We were forced to leave our comfortable

life full of love from my maternal family and go forth into a foreign land. It was a fearsome and adrenaline-filled time, especially for me at a very young age. Yet God had His hand on every member of my family; He had a divine purpose for each of our lives. We did not understand why God had chosen this path for our lives at the time, but we never seemed to waver. God was always in control. We had no choice but to keep our eyes on God in prayer and hope that there was some purpose in the challenges we faced.

Is it not high time we break the silence? God hears us when we cry out and sees the tears on our cheeks. He will hear you if only you trust Him. Watch God guide you to your purpose. Your success is scheduled because God knew you even before you were conceived in your mother's womb.

There have been all types of detours in my life and perhaps in yours as well. But I assure you that as long as you proclaim, "Here I am, Lord," you are right on time.

It is the hour for all people, young and old, to be bold enough to share their testimonies. It is time to make it happen just as the last book of the Bible declares, "They triumphed over him by the blood of the Lamb and by the word of their testimony; they did not love their lives so much as to shrink from death" (Revelation

12:11 NIV). What an encouragement to us to avail ourselves of God wherever we are.

Let Him use you in hard times as well as in good times. It started for me with a solid foundation in God that was imparted to me through my family values.

CHAPTER 2

Family Values

Several values come to mind when I think of my family. I consider respect, prayer, discipline, education, simplicity, and humor to be deeply embedded in my family and in our Zimbabwean culture alike. My parents and extended family have directly and indirectly reflected these six values in my life. I think of the saying, "It takes a village to raise a child." They had helped form my character by grounding me in my culture, which was especially needed when I became an African immigrant growing up in the United States.

Respect

When I think of my family, the word *respect* comes first to mind. In my culture, you are taught to respect your elders, your peers, and yourself. If you deviate from that, you disrespect yourself, your peers, and your elders. Not illustrating that you are cultured shows you have refused to listen to counsel or have disgraced your parents. In Shona, this is called *tsika*.

For example, elders should not be found doing tedious chores if younger people are able to handle them. You should never let your mom cook while you sit and watch if you are old enough to help her. I specifically recall how we greeted adults when entering a house—we would kneel before my grandparents, uncles, and aunties and clap as an official, respectful greeting (*kuombera*). Males kneel and clap with their hands cupped slightly in a diamond shape; females kneel and clap with their hands cuffed in a zigzag shell shape.

Prayer

I was born the daughter of a woman of prayer. My mother, aunties, and grandmother are all prayer warriors. Naturally, Mama taught me how to pray. It was and still is a way of life for me. The day I stop seeking God in prayer, generations after me will be affected. As such, I look forward to the day I will have children and impart a mother's blessing through prayer, which changes things.

Living in the United States, I am nothing without God and need to communicate with my Creator regularly. Sure, I am not perfect and may forget to do a morning prayer when I wake up, but I know my heavenly Father is waiting for me to stop even amid the chaos of life and say, "Here I am, Lord!"

Discipline

Discipline provides family structure and rules of behavior; parents and elders teach and admonish us. Essentially, we have to maintain a meticulous mind-set to work hard enough for our aspirations; we cannot simply depend on others' efforts.

As a child, I observed how hardworking my parents were. My father and mother got ready for work daily like clockwork. I am sure Mama could have decided to be a stay-at-home mom if she had desired, but she was a working mom—she would come back and coordinate dinner, and she would check my brother's and my homework. If we were sick, she would pray for us, make sure we got to bed on time, and repeat the routine the next day. That took orderliness and persistent effort.

Education

Education is so greatly valued in my culture and family. My maternal grandparents demonstrated that by sending their children and other people's children to school. My maternal grandmother was a teacher, and all my uncles and aunts pursued higher education.

My parents had met in university; both were studying accounting. My father went on to complete a master's degree and a PhD in public administration, and he continues to acquire professional financial certifications today. My mother once jokingly told him, "Leave some learning for the rest of us!"

I love my parents; they taught me to never stop learning.

Simplicity

I keep one of my favorite quotations from Albert Einstein as a screen saver on my laptop: "Everything should be made as simple as possible, but not simpler." Too often, we complicate life by not keeping things simple. We should desire good things but live within our means. My mother taught me that, and I thank her for that.

Sometimes on Sundays after church, the family would come home and share a meal. As an adult in the States, I loved walking trails with my mom on beautiful, sunny, fall days. One particular day, we finished walking a trail through a nearby forest. Instead of jumping back in the car and returning home, we walked toward this well-nourished tree. It had huge branches, and my five-six self attempted to jump and grab one. Mama, being five seven with long arms, barely left the ground to grab a branch and said, "If someone spots us leaping for these branches, they'll think both of us have problems!" It was at moments like that that Mama would counsel me and explain life's principles. She taught me, "Be simple, be practical, be ambitious, but always be you."

Humor

Zimbabweans have a way of laughing their way through life's challenges. Laughter is a medicine and way of life. Being able to laugh at life's troubles belittles those problems so you do not stress out on them and get old too quickly.

At so many times, anyone observing us might have marveled at how my family and I were coping as African immigrants in America. We were fighting battles on numerous fronts including visa challenges. At times, the gravity of family issues was so spiritually traumatic that it was only through a healing process that we could laugh after. All the same, the joy of the Lord was our source of strength in all things!

CHAPTER 3

Grandparents

People do not realize how much of childhood cultivates their character until they are older. Most of us cannot remember times in our lives before we were four or five, but photos can jog our memories. Even more important are our emotions—what we felt about critical incidents in our past and how other people made us feel. I remember particularly how my grandparents made me feel.

Mama would always dress me up in these prissy, A-line dresses my father bought for me. I would look picture perfect, especially on Sunday mornings heading to church. My hair often mimicked Minnie Mouse's buns with accompanying red ribbons.

After attending Sunday service, Mama would drive us to my maternal grandparents' house in Marlborough, a short drive from

Harare, Zimbabwe's capital. We spent much time there. As far back as I can remember, when I got to Marlborough, all my uncles and aunts would greet me by my nickname, "Mukadzi Mutsvuku!" (light-skinned lady).

My maternal grandfather gave me that nickname that still resonates with me today. Sekuru Kavayi was light skinned as well; he had a much lighter skin tone than did I. He was a well-respected, successful businessman and farmer who had much authority by training and inclination. He was a God-fearing man who cared for people whether related to him or not; he often paid for many children's school fees.

On so many visits to Marlborough, I would enter the living room and spot Sekuru Kavayi seated in his wooden rocking chair. If it was toward the end of the day, the rays of the sun would catch the left side of his face. Sekuru Kavayi was a gentleman who carried an aura of serenity.

Comparably, my maternal grandmother had the ability to light up any room she entered. Gogo Kavayi (Gogo being a common name for grandma in Shona) was a God-fearing woman. She was a woman of impeccable character, a teacher by profession and a Mother's Union leader and counselor at St. Paul's Anglican Church. Gogo loved to sing in the choir, and when we visited her, we would be sure to sing a few hymns.

She was the mother of nine children and the grandmother to countless cousins and my siblings and me. Gogo Kavayi nurtured generations by challenging us always to serve God wherever we found ourselves in life.

In 2012, when I was twenty-one, she was still spoiling me. We went to the capital city market, and Gogo, who was seventy-eight, would occasionally stop and ask me, "Do you want a banana?" or "Shall I buy you a drink?"

I cherish the memory of those simple moments with her. I also cherish her delicious cooking. One of my favorites she used to make for me as a child was *nhopi*, mashed pumpkin or butternut squash mixed with peanut butter. I have always been a sucker for *dovi*, peanut butter; a lot of Zimbabwean food goes with it such as rice, spinach, collard greens, and even porridge. No one's nhopi is better than Gogo's.

I knew I would miss her dearly as my 2012 trip to see her was coming to an end. On the last day, Gogo spoke some very profound words of life over me. I was to catch an afternoon flight to the United States to finish my last year of undergraduate studies. Time felt like it slowed down when Gogo sat on her sofa and looked at me. I looked at her anticipating what she would tell me. It was this: "May the Lord bless you for the good work you are doing. Keep doing well in school and supporting the church you attend. You are a leader, and you will prosper."

I will never forget that moment; Gogo saw something in me I had yet to understand completely, but she had the gift of discernment. She blessed me, and for that, I am reaping the benefits as the words of life she sowed in me are manifesting.

Sometimes, I wish I had more memories of my paternal grandparents, or to be quite honest, more concrete, happy thoughts about them. Since childhood, I unfortunately have never reminisced about my paternal grandparents. From what I recall and from what my mom told me, Daddy's father was a decent, loving man who loved to sing his Methodist hymns. He passed away suddenly from cancer of the throat when I was six, so I do not have much recollection of him.

At the other end of the spectrum, my paternal grandmother made me feel like prey. So many emotions run through my head when she comes to mind. She put my family and me through immense stress and emotional pain. On rare occasions, I have enjoyable recollections of her. The only moderately funny memory that actually stemmed from envy is when she visited our family in our home in Greendale, Zimbabwe. She entered the house through the garage and saw a cute black duffle bag in the corner. It belonged to one of the painters we had hired to do some work on our house. She insisted on taking it with her and repeatedly asked who it belonged to. We never answered her question or gave her the bag, but we secretly gave her the nickname "ChiBagi."

Otherwise, fond memories of my father's mother are close to none, but I have learned to forgive her. By God's orchestration, time has taught me to forgive her, but that forgiveness did not happen all at once; it came in phases.

People often tell us to forgive anyone who has hurt us; this is a biblical injunction found in multiple scriptures such as, "Be kind and compassionate to one another, forgiving each other, just as in Christ God forgave you" (Ephesians 4:32 NIV). But we forget that genuine forgiveness is accomplished only in phases. When others offend us whether in a trivial or serious way, can we say we forgave the person immediately and resumed the relationship as before?

Being authentic to your feelings but still and forgiving others requires strength from God and faith in Him to truly heal as required by the scriptures. First, we must establish a firm decision to forgive. Although that can challenge our faith and character, taking that first step will lead us to liberation and healing.

Second, we cannot forgive someone from our strength alone; we ought to practice our faith by prayerfully asking God to help us so we do not pray in the flesh with anger. Remember, we decide to forgive to obey God and be able to live in peace.

Third, depending on the depth of the pain we experience, we will feel all kinds of emotions;

we have to recognize this so our emotions do not cause us to act out of character. Every time we give into our anger increases the time it will take us to heal. Just because we decided to forgive does not mean our pain immediately goes away. It is natural for our decision to forgive to be way ahead of our ability to do so.

Last, and what I believe to be the hardest phase of forgiveness, is the will to pray for those who have caused you pain. This phase of forgiveness requires you to put into practice all my previous suggestions. Make a conscious decision to forgive, pray to God for strength, keep your emotions in check, and pray for those who caused you pain.

All my grandparents made me feel various emotions that have affected my character. Even the negative and uncategorized emotions that call for forgiveness have molded me in tremendous ways as a woman of God today. My writing this book is a testimony to the stages of forgiveness I have gone through to relieve the sting and some of my life's deepest hurts.

CHAPTER 4

Brotherly Love

I love my older brother with whom I spent so much time. Gary looked out for me, and I had his back too. Well, most of the time.

When we visited Gogo's house, we looked forward to playing outside with my cousins. On occasion, one of us would get hurt or some other mishap would take place. Just beyond our uncles' garage was an old shell of a car with very few interior parts and no wheels. Being kids and completely ignoring the fact that it could be dangerous, a few of my cousins and I climbed into the car. I sat in the driver's seat pretending to be racing what used to be a car. I pulled the steering wheel to the left and the right. I stepped on the gas pedal and yelled, "*Vruum! Vrumm!*" I pretended I was making the car skid just as my uncles, who raced at Zimbabwe's Donnybrook raceway, did by stomping on the brake pedal. I froze. Everyone else was fooling around. It took big brother Gary to rescue me. There was no brake pedal; what was left of it was a nail sticking up that had pierced my foot.

I suppose I was in shock. My foot was utterly numb. Gary held my right leg tight and pulled the rusted nail out. The pain caught up to my shock, and the waterworks erupted. But instead of calling for an adult in the house, Gary and my cousins comforted me; they wanted me to stop crying before everyone got in trouble.

After a while, I limped back to the house hiding behind Gary. Of course, mothers know their children, Mama noticed I was limping and eventually discovered what had taken place almost an hour earlier.

Everyone's immediate intuition was to blame Gary; that prompted my cousins to coin the phrase "*Ndi Gary!*" "It was Gary!"

Another incident occurred on a laid-back Saturday at Gogo's house when I was with a lot of my cousins. My uncle Sekuru Admire had a collection of cartoons on VHS tapes in his room for his nieces and nephews as well as himself. A favorite was *The Lion King*. Though all of us had watched that film about fifty times, he knew it would distract us for a bit while he worked on his cars and motorcycles in the garage. So there I was with my cousins watching Simba fighting Mufasa once again as if we did not know who would win the battle. We did not realize my cousin Tawanda and Gary had gone missing in action.

Thirty minutes later, we spotted Uncle Admire, Sekuru Admire, through one of the living room windows running with a bucket of water in one hand; hanging off his shoulder was a rolled-up water hose. Puzzled at what was taking place, my cousins and I rushed outside. We reached the back of Gogo's kitchen yard and witnessed the five-foot-something-tall bushes on fire! They were not regular bushes; they were more of a decorative garden wall that lined the houses' driveway toward the end of the property to Sekuru Admire's garage. "Ndi Gary and Tawanda!" we all exclaimed!

When the other adults returned to the house from their walk, they asked the two boys what they were trying to do. Their response was, "We saw a wasp inside the bush and tried to burn it with matches!"

Though Gary and Tawanda got into loads of trouble for that, we still laugh at that incident and others today. Like when I was six and playing with Gary at our Greendale home during school break. Gary walked up to me and said, "Let's go to Tawanda's house!"

Without questioning how we were going to get there or asking if any adults knew of Gary's schemes, I said, "Okay." Mind you, I didn't know how to maneuver my way on public transportation at that age, but Gary, who was eleven, seemed confident. He grabbed my hand and led me to the nearest kombi bus stop just outside the Greendale neighborhood.

In Zimbabwe, private fifteen-passenger vans are called *kombis*. If you were lucky, the one you got in would have only about seventeen people; that would have been a comfortable ride.

Gary got us to the west side of Marlborough by foot, and then we boarded a kombi for the thirty-two-minute ride (twenty-five kilometers, about fifteen miles). Where Gary had gotten the money to pay for the kombi was another question, but we sure had fun that day playing soccer and Mortal Kombat on Tawanda's Sega Geniuses game system. We didn't think of the consequences of our trip.

Once my aunt, Maiguru Mai Farai, learned we were at her house, she immediately called Mama. "Did you know Gary is here kuMarlborough?" Baffled, my mother drove to get us and gave it to Gary. When she looked at me, all I could say in my cutest, most-innocent voice was, "Ndi Gary!"

Gary was the firstborn son in my immediate family. I listened to whatever he told me to do without question. He has always been more into sports than academics. Even the primary school we attended couldn't help make him a prefect for grades six and seven despite his trips to the headmaster. His playful but continuous misbehavior led him to start wearing double shorts under his primary school uniform so it wouldn't hurt as much when the headmaster would give him lashes. (That form of discipline was allowed in our culture as well as in schools then.)

That did not halt Gary's popularity; everyone liked his charismatic personality. They nicknamed him "Gaz" as he won freestyle swimming, cross-country, and track and field races. He was the school's sports legend in soccer, cricket, and rugby. I am sure with a little less mischief and more focus, Gaz could have represented the Zimbabwe national team in the sport of his choice. He was a slim, fit, six-two force to be reckoned with in just about any sport I know of. It didn't bother me that schoolmates could not remember my name and would just ask me, "Hey, you're Gaz's little sister, right?" Yes I was.

At home, he wouldn't let me rest until I helped him with his cricket game by being the batter while he balled. I was barely tall enough to hold the heavy cricket bat, but I would do anything Gary asked, and we would listen to Michael Jackson's greatest hits Gary had blasting through our Greendale living room speakers. Another secret I kept from Mama.

I adored my older brother, which is why what happened to him devastated everyone. Gary wasn't okay.

CHAPTER 5

Simukai (Rise Up)

I had many childhood memories living in our Greendale home. My parents had worked hard in their professions and designed the blueprints for our house. Brick by brick, they built their dream home. It was where I most recall Gary and I being raised. Unfortunately, in many African cultures and elsewhere, having good things in your life can attract envy—jealous, green eyes that watch your happiness and wonder why they do not have what you have been blessed with.

What baffles me is that people forget that God gives us all gifts and talents and the strength to work. As much as a man of God can pour oil on our heads, pray, and prophesy about our lives, we must work: "The one who is unwilling to work shall not eat" (2 Thessalonians 3:10 NIV). Nothing happens if you say you have faith but don't apply yourself and do what you have to do.

My parents, who were in their thirties, had two kids and excellent corporate jobs. They owned a five-bedroom dream house with a separate cottage, and they had a future to fight for.

Mama had been offered a scholarship to earn a master's degree at a university in La Verne, California. How exciting, right? But she was worried about how difficult it would be to leave her family and children to go to school there. By that time, our family was enjoying the addition of my younger brother, TJ. However, the scholarship recommended to my mother by my aunt, Maiguru Mai Anesu, could not go to waste. So my wise mother encouraged my father to apply for it instead of her and take the opportunity while she nursed TJ.

My parents met two professors who were visiting Zimbabwe looking for possible candidates. I remember peeking into our Greendale living room and seeing the two visitors speaking with my parents. To the left was one Caucasian female and to the right one African-American male. *They talk funny*, I thought as I listened in on the conversation. It was the first time I had heard an American accent in person. That meeting changed the course of our lives.

After going back and forth with the

university's admissions office on the phone, Daddy almost gave up. He had submitted his letter of resignation at work and been home a month waiting on his F-1 student visa the male professor had promised he would receive. My mother took charge; she called to find out just what the delay was. She spoke to a sweet admissions representative who was surprised to hear that my father was still waiting for the visa. "The professor you met and conversed with came back from Zimbabwe and told us you didn't want the scholarship anymore!"

Surprised and shocked, my mother thought, *What a destiny killer!* The male professor had seen how well my parents had done for themselves in their lovely Greendale home and had taken it upon himself to decide my father's future. Immediately, Mama set the record straight—my dad was coming to California and needed just the visa. You see, this life is a journey, and even if unnamed forces are trying to divert you from your predetermined path, God will intercept you on your detour.

So there I was months later knowing full well that Daddy was in the United States studying. But my mother told my paternal uncle Jake that my father had gone to South Africa on a work trip. Like a lioness, she was protecting her cubs and pride.

Our family was on pretend-friendly terms

with a few relatives on my father's side for the sake of peace. Daddy had been the prominent son and brother who through hard work was known for having been an executive at several businesses and organizations. He was a member of the Chartered Accountants of Zimbabwe after graduating from the University of Zimbabwe with a bachelor's degree in accountancy (with honors). He had done well in school; he knew that would be his gateway to a life that was better than the one he had come from. Education was not valued in his family, but Daddy certainly valued it.

When he had settled down and married my mother, he named his firstborn Simukai Garikai. *Simukai* means to rise, to get up and rise above your current condition. Sometimes, your environment can weigh you down and unconsciously give you a mind-set that hinders you from achieving a better life or new heights. *Garikai* means "to live well" as in a blessed life without strife. Those were his first and middle names.

Daddy had witnessed so many family conflicts on multiple fronts that he did not want that anymore. It wasn't the most conventional way of dealing with the situation, but we tried to use wisdom in dealing with such characters on my father's side. They were aggravated that they did not know Daddy was out of the country or when he would return.

Why did they need him so much? Because he was the prominent son and brother who could also finance their lives' habits. On many occasions, my father had paid for them to go to school so they could become self-sufficient and live decent lives, but that gesture was considered showing off or arrogant. In Shona, we call this *kudada*. But some of my extended paternal family did not see that Daddy was trying to teach them how to fish rather than continuously feeding them fish. He could not be their breadwinner forever.

Their questions increased; their requests to speak to my father became demands. They thought my mother had convinced Daddy not to be there to finance their children's school fees or pay for whatever they wanted. I believe it started with their insecurity; they were not taking God's Word into consideration.

Insecurity is naturally a part of life, and we all experience it at times. However, it needs to be monitored and dealt with appropriately because it can cause us to entertain unhealthy thoughts. When we continuously entertain negative thoughts, the devil begins to sow deceitful seeds in our minds. It is one of the most common tricks he plays on us, so it is important for us to guard our thoughts. We can do that by reminding ourselves who we are in Christ, praying, and declaring the Word of God over our lives.

If we don't renew our minds daily in this fashion by putting on the helmet of salvation, our unhealthy thoughts will develop into jealousy, which can turn into envy. We can start questioning why other people are better off than we are. The enemy uses that to get us angry about where we are in life and to prompt us to act on devious thoughts.

If you are not in Christ or you avail yourself in that negative manner, you become a slave to the enemy. Satan will use you in his war against the children of God. Romans 6:20–23 best touches on how we are all slaves to sin until we are set free by God's gift of eternal life in Christ Jesus to seek after righteousness. God gives us all free will to choose to sin or put on righteousness. The full armor of God is what we ought to put on daily. "Righteousness will be his belt and faithfulness the sash around his waist." (Isaiah 11:5 NIV)

It is unfortunate that relatives or those closest to you can be your adversaries who try to pull you down instead of supporting you for the betterment of everyone. The coalition of family that opposed us decided to turn to what lost, unsaved, and primitive individuals look to when they want to manipulate people, their lives, and well-being—witchcraft.

Who would be their victim to convince my father to return from supposedly South Africa and give them what they needed? Ndi Gary.

That is not how we had wanted to use that term. Attacking Gary, my father's firstborn, would cause the most emotional and physical harm and pain so that they could get their way.

Daddy had to be frugal when he was studying in the United States. Mama decided to rent out our lovely Greendale family dream house and move into a more-compact, three-bedroom flat. The relocation helped her save money, and she occasionally changed Zimbabwean dollars into U.S. dollars via Western Union. Yes, once upon a time, that was feasible. Now, the Zimbabwean dollar does not exist, but that's another whole story. But the coalition did not see our move to Letombo Park as a healthy development. Instead, our move heightened the tension as they inquired why we were selling furniture and moving out of the house. Frequent visits to monitor when Daddy was coming back became more than uncomfortable.

So there I was, getting ready to go to Ariel School and my beloved older brother to his secondary school, Prince Edward. Despite Gary's academic performance, he got accepted into Prince Edward, a prominent high school. We were all so happy for him. Gary was stoked; he talked about the sports he was likely to play such as soccer, cricket, and rugby. We had been an inseparable pair, but

Gary would be going to school without his sidekick sister.

Fully settled in the Letombo Park flat, I remember taking a bath one morning and putting on my clean ironed school uniform so I could catch the large charter bus leaving Greendale for Ariel School in Ruwa, a rural area; my primary school sat on what was a large farm. The school was in the news once. When Gary and I were still attending the same school, a strange event took place. The media reported some students had spotted UFOs. You can still find the story on an old 1996 video that someone later uploaded to YouTube. Gary claims he saw something till this day, but that is a whole other book if I go there.

It was the first few weeks of the beginning of a new school year in 1999. I had some spare time to catch the bus and Gary his. I had already eaten some porridge for breakfast. Gary was nowhere to be seen. As I walked to his room, I heard a loud shriek and commotion in the bathroom. Mama rushed toward the bathroom and opened the door. I quickly followed her. Mama found Gary almost drowning in the bathtub. She helped him pull himself up; he looked as if he were wrestling something.

Just as she managed to help him lean against the tub, Gary fell unconscious. Mama paused for a moment probably thinking the same thing I was: *What's going on?* Mama and Sisi, who was our maid, attempted to wake him up, but he wouldn't. He was breathing but he seemed to be in a coma. Moments later, he became conscious but was still sitting in the bathtub yelling, "Mama!"

"We're here, Gary. What's going on?"

Gary shrieked, "I see women all around me! They're singing, laughing, and saying your father must come back home or else you are going to die!"

He fell unconscious again. That went on for another few minutes, and he awoke again. "Mama, I cannot see! I can't see anything!"

Gary could hear us, but he was blind.

Standing beside Sisi and behind Mama, I was petrified. I had never seen anything like that in my young seven years, and I was deeply disturbed. I recall Mama making an urgent call to someone and instructing the maid to begin praying. As they prayed, Mama told me to get my school bag so she could drive me to school because I had missed my regular bus. Not fully understanding that my brother had just been spiritually attacked, I hopped into the car. Mama speedily drove me to school about fifteen miles away, and she rushed home to Gary. I couldn't think. I was in shock. Gary was not okay.

CHAPTER 6

Who Can Help Us?

The conjuring attack was unforgivable. Gary's names meant, "rise and live well," but the opposite was occurring. Gary stopped going to school; the spiritual attack continued. He could not wake up. He remained in a coma-like state. He had been doing so well in sports, he was doing his best academically, and he had such a bright future. The Bible says our enemies can be people in our families. That was proven true by some of our extended paternal family. It is unfathomable that your own blood can go to such extents. For what exactly? Maybe for money, control, manipulation, or jealousy? This bewitchment was wickedness at its highest level.

When I returned home, Mama was there; she had not gone to work. She explained to me as best as she could that Gary had woken up only well after school hours. Whoever was behind this had invoked evil spirits to stop Gary from waking up in the morning and kept him in that state until school was over.

These spiritual attacks continued if almost every other day if not every day. They were designed to disturb Gary's studies and bring Daddy back to Zimbabwe.

Mama decided to tell my extended maternal family about all this, and we took Gary to Gogo's house in Marlborough. I distinctly remember that Saturday evening; it was not as jolly and carefree as usual. We all sat in the living room and sang hymns in Shona. My mother, uncles, aunts, and Gogo all prayed for Gary. When Mama drove home, I thought, *I hope this week, things will get better.* But they didn't.

Monday morning, I dreaded walking down the hallway to Gary's room. Mama and Sisi were standing outside Gary's door. "It's locked," Sisi said as I approached. I had woken up earlier than usual; no one was sleeping those days. I had time before my bus came. Mama was not in her work clothes, but she marched outside to peer into Gary's bedroom window. Mama looked inside Gary's room, and sure enough, he was lying on his bed in the same coma-like state. We banged and knocked on the window, but he wouldn't wake up. Gary did not usually lock his bedroom door.

I had to hurry to catch my bus. At seven years old, I was seeing so many spiritual things and events around me; I was struggling to take it all in. Once I got on the bus, although not sleepy, I closed my eyes. "Everything is going to be alright," I whispered softly to myself.

Some neighborhood students who knew Gary would ask me, "Hey, where's Gaz?" He had been missing a lot school. I couldn't respond to them. I became extra quiet. I was in fourth grade. I heard my teachers talking, but I was mentally absent from the lesson. It began to reflect in my grades, but it just didn't seem as important as what was going on at home. I missed my older brother; I wanted him better and whole again. I missed playing outside with him or watching his school sports competitions as before.

My report card was due. The teacher told me I was not doing too well and asked if everything was okay. I said nothing. Then the terrible report card was mailed home, and I contemplated forging Mama's signature so she did not have to deal with my teacher or me. Consequently, I think the teacher picked up on something and arranged a parent-teacher meeting.

I sat there between Mama on my right and the teacher on my left. The teacher explained how my performance had declined and said that I seemed to be thinking a lot. She asked

Mama, "Is everything okay?" Knowing exactly what was affecting me, Mama burst into tears. Mama and I were so sad, but my teacher was clueless as to why. The school put me in a class where they would try to help me learn better and improve my grades.

An entirely different set of events took place on weekends. We were looking for help. Gary continued to suffer from spiritual attacks, and Daddy remained in the States understanding the situation but not physically seeing the gravity of everything for himself. We spent Saturdays going to see praying men referred to as *mapostori* in Shona. After they would pray for Gary, they would reaffirm that a few individuals from our extended paternal family were behind the spiritual attacks.

We visited another praying family friend who was more forthright; he told us, "It's the father's mother." That was not a big shock. That woman was behind Gary's afflictions someway, somehow. She wanted Daddy to come back so he would do whatever she wanted.

We continued searching for help. One time, one of my mother's aunts went with us. I had no idea where we were going. It was getting dark. Mama was driving, her aunt was in the passenger seat, and Gary and I were in the back. We must have left TJ at Gogo's house because I do not recall him being with us then. We drove up to a hut in a rural area. I remember the moonlight shining brightly that night. I also remember being terrified of a turkey waiting for me to get out of the car. I was only about four feet tall, and that bird looked towering when I sprinted out of the car.

We entered one of the grass-roofed huts. The people inside were seated quietly staring at the fireplace in the center. It was quite smoky. *Why are we here?* I asked myself. Feeling rather sleepy, I sat next to Mama. The man who seemed to carry some authority looked at Mama and made a statement that stuck with all of us that night. Translating the overarching meaning in English, he spoke in Shona and reassured my mother, "Listen, all the stuff we do is limited. You, ma'am, keep on praying and seeking your God. One day, you will look back, and it will be as if you hardly remember all these spiritual attacks and trials."

I only later understood that the man was a herbalist or something like that. We were seeking help wherever we could find it. Desperate life challenges can push you to do that. Even all those alternatives were recommending Jesus. By human standards, few could have overcome and survived what had happened to Gary. It seemed hopeless, and even other praying women from my mother's church had written Gary's case off as a lost cause. They were not the only ones; many expected soon to hear that the boy had gotten worse or had even passed away.

CHAPTER 7

We Left the Stove On!

I had spent my Saturday afternoon trying to do what most eight-year-olds did in their free time. The morning was filled with helping Sisi clean out my room and hang my washed school uniform on the laundry line just outside the kitchen. My mother and the maid could spot me playing on the small yard outside of our Letombo Park flat front yard. I preferred the front yard though the backyard was more spacious and private. Perhaps it was the quick access to the street that would allow me to watch the latest neighborhood drama or quickly hop on my red BMX bicycle.

Playing outside was one of my happy places. It made me feel like all the ordinary kids. Sometimes, I joined a neighborhood soccer game in the street and climbed trees. Once, I even attempted to fly off a four-foot brick barbecue stand using pieces of cardboard as wings. My mother would scold me; she'd tell me girls didn't climb trees or anything else for that matter. I seemed not to have learned my lesson from the previous year when I received a nasty wound that cut me from my knee down my leg; twelve stitches had been required. The doctor asked me if I had been trying to fly. Ironically, I had actually been singing R Kelly's "I believe I can fly."

It was time to head inside as sunset was nearing. I had exerted a lot of energy that day and was ready for a bath. After cleaning up, I went into the living room to watch *Jeopardy* on TV. Sisi had started supper. I smelled *sadza* simmering on the stove, beef stew, and fresh-cut cabbage. Sadza in Shona is a cooked cornmeal, a staple food in Zimbabwe. Every household partakes of *sadza nenyama nemuriwo* (meat and leafy vegetables) almost every day be it lunch or dinner. Gary was listening to music. I was trying to get his attention so we could play Crazy 8s, my favorite card game, which Sisi had taught us. With luck, I would beat Gary despite our age gap of five years. TJ, my younger brother, had started attempting to walk a bit. A step here and there and an occasional outburst, but he was trotting once in a while across the living room. Everything seemed normal.

Let me see what Mama is doing, I thought.

My mother was sitting on her bed in the master bedroom. I noticed the fan was off despite it being a dry season and a summer night. I suppose it was only natural considering what had taken place a couple of weeks earlier.

Almost a month prior, I had been watching my mother change TJ's diaper on the bed. While in motion at the end of the day's hustle and bustle, she had swung her right arm up not minding her tall height. Mama screamed! I was frightened.

"Mama, chi? What's wrong?" I asked.

"My hand! Oh my goodness!"

The fan had badly sliced one of Mama's fingers. I saw blood gushing from it. I rushed to grab the first aid kit for alcohol and bandages.

"Sorry, Mama, sorry." I tried to comfort her. I wondered what Daddy would have done if he had been there. He would have known what to do to make her feel better. He would have protected her. But Daddy had been gone for what seemed like ages.

Our family had always been together—Daddy, Mama, Gary, me, and TJ. Daddy would take us on fun road trips and vacations to Victoria Falls, Lake Kariba, Matopos Hills, and even Great Zimbabwe, which had been Zimbabwe's capital when it was a kingdom during the country's late fifteenth-century iron age and the location of the royal palace.

Daddy's fun trips instilled a sense of adventure in me. I understood traveling as a family thing even when I was very young. So why had Daddy left us alone and not taken us with him? He had left in a rush; Daddy should have been here to protect Mama. I felt some resentment toward my father because he should have been here to protect us all.

Mama would remind me that Daddy had traveled to the United States to study for a master's degree. Without questioning other events taking place around me, I took my mother's explanation at face value.

So there I was reminiscing and still standing in the doorway of Mama's master bedroom. I walked into her room. "Mama, what are you doing?" Her room always smelled so fresh and clean. I suppose she had just finished taking a shower.

"I'm coming. Let's go eat sadza," she said. I could tell she was tired and stressed. However, my mother always had a way of providing such comfort even when you knew things were not all straightforward. Again, I pondered wishful thoughts of Daddy.

We were all in the living room about to gather to pray over the food. A pot of beef stew was still simmering on the stove.

"Ah! Mama, I see two people walking toward the house!" Sisi yelled.

Everyone turned their attention to the

kitchen. Mama burst into the kitchen to understand why Sisi was alarmed. She found Sisi leaning over the kitchen counter and staring out the window. What two people would be walking toward the front of our house at that time? We were not expecting any visitors, especially those days where unusual events had been occurring.

Sisi stared at Mama with big, shocked eyes, "Ndi ChiBagi Mama! ChiBagi *nemumwe murume!*" "ChiBagi and another man."

"ChiBagi!" Mama repeated.

Everyone including Mama was astounded. Without hesitation, Mama ordered everyone to grab a few things and head out the door that led to our backyard. "Switch off the lights, *Handei!* Let's go!" she said.

Sisi followed orders and switched off the kitchen lights first and sprinted to the living room lights. I had a jacket in hand and was headed out the backdoor. Gary also had one or two things in hand, and Mama was holding TJ with a toddler's bag hanging off her shoulder.

By divine orchestration, Mama had parked her car at the rear of the house; it wasn't visible from the front yard. We all swiftly made our way to the car. Mama started the engine and began to reverse in neutral. It was as if we were training for a military stealth exercise. We had gotten out of the house in less than a minute.

Sisi jumped in the car last; we were all running on adrenaline.

"Stop, Mirai, Stop!" Sisi said. "We left the beef stew pot on the stove on!"

"Run! Go switch it off and just bring the pot with you!" Mama ordered.

There were so many moving parts in that minute, but by the grace of God, we had escaped ChiBagi and the accompanying man.

As Mama drove off using back roads, everyone in the car started breathing easier the farther we were from Letombo Park. We headed to a safe place, Marlborough, where my maternal grandmother lived, another one of my happy places that made me feel like the average kid.

Between Sisi and Mama's grown-up conversation in the car, I deduced that the mysterious man was Uncle Jake. I also knew that ChiBagi was the code name for my paternal grandmother. Yes, in the middle of the night, Sisi, my family, and I were running away from my paternal uncle and grandmother to seek haven at my maternal grandmother's house. The aroma of beef stew filled my mother's 1990 white Mazda 323 sedan. Nothing was normal.

CHAPTER 8

Hoping

One bright, sunny day, I was approaching my school bus stop. Habit, what I call muscle memory, had kicked in and was guiding me along the quickest way to get there from our Letombo Park flat. It was my routine to take the opportunity to reflect on Gary, my family, and the overarching spiritual chaos I was witnessing. I lifted my head to the bright, blue sky and embraced the warmth of the morning sun. For the first time, I took notice of humongous tropical palm trees that neatly lined the Greendale neighborhood streets. They reminded me of the movies set in California I used to watch with Gary.

"One day, I will go to California," I whispered to myself. I am sure if other students were looking at me, they would have concluded me not to be all correct upstairs. But I didn't care.

Though I was just eight, I knew that some way, somehow, God would make everything all right. I felt the comforting presence of God in the warmth and in the beautiful Zimbabwean sky. It was only later, when I was an adult, that I fully understood what I was doing in that moment. It was a spark of hope. I was proclaiming things that were not as though they were. I was looking to the hills where my help came from.

Our help comes from the Lord, the maker of heaven and earth.

I was walking by faith of a child and not by sight.

I was hoping for a better tomorrow.

I was hoping for my older brother to be healed.

I was hoping for my whole family to be together once again.

I was hoping I could enjoy what most eight-year-olds focus on, for I had seen a lot of spiritual things and had held onto my childlike faith.

There were good days and weeks as well as terrifying times when Gary could not wake up for school or go to church on the weekends. It was as if our perpetrators knew we were praying and were trying to stop anything we tried to help him and disturb the power of God that was keeping us all. But God's power cannot be restricted to a church building or any other physical structure. The more we prayed, the more the spiritual attacks intensified. Sometimes, Gary would have dreams; Mama and I would sometimes have them too. I experienced a strange recurring nightmare and knew not what it meant, but I kept praying with my family. I would dread going to sleep, but when I did, the dream would begin.

I was in a room by myself. No people, no physical structure, just unknown space surrounding me. Every time I took a step, I saw strange colors that changed the ambiance of the area. I made another movement, and the colors changed faster and faster. A bit anxious and frightened for not knowing where I was or what was taking place, I tried calling out, "Help, Mama! Help!" But I couldn't make a sound. The strange colors turned into a complex, moving pattern. The dream would usually end with me waking up from my dream screaming out for Mama.

To this day, I feel those dreams were intended to confuse me at school and become disturbed like Gary. However, even as a child, I had a stubborn spirit, and that is what it takes to resist the devil.

I returned home that day after having my smiling-with-God session earlier that morning at the bus stop. Mama told me that Gary had a rugby match we were going to watch. In the midst of storms, we tried our best to enjoy pleasant moments when we could.

Christmas came, and of course we spent it with extended maternal family at Gogo's house in Marlborough. New Year's Eve and Day lifted our spirits. Unfortunately, it did not have the same effect on ChiBagi, Uncle Jake, and the other members of the coalition. It had been almost six months, and they were taking the absence of my father personally. They had been used to my dad dropping whatever he was doing with his wife and children to appease their financial requests and devious agendas. "Baba Simukai must return!" became their repeated slogan.

The coalition championed this theme with persistent trips to consult evil shenanigans and to put to work whatever fiendish means they could. I felt that the spiritual world was so much in my face, and I knew without a doubt that God was real. How could we have survived an entire year of these attacks had it not been for God's protection in the midst of chaos?

The following weekend, Mama rushed Gary, TJ, and me to Greatermans, a modern shopping mall in Harare. We got there not knowing what to expect. A gentleman with a commercial camera greeted us. He took

Gary's, Mama's, and TJ's pictures. When he got to me, I gave a quick smile knowing my hair was short; Mama had just cut it. I do not remember why. Perhaps I had overpermed it because that was the hair fad those days.

I realized only days later that the pictures were for passport photos. My parents had spoken on the phone and agreed to Daddy's instruction for Mama to quickly get the family ready to come to the United States. Daddy had filed the immigration paperwork to sponsor all of us in the United States with H-1 visas. By divine orchestration, our visas were approved in unconventional record time. Another miracle.

Mama made arrangements for our tenant's rental payments to be sent to us. She quit her job and career; she left behind everything she had built in life. We told no one about our travel plans except for my maternal family, who prayed for us. Everything happened so quickly. Bags were packed. I dressed in a gray jean jacket and pants outfit on the day we were leaving. How is that for late-nineties fashion? It ironically had a bald eagle on the back of the jacket, the same eagle on a U.S. quarter and America's national symbol of liberty.

We hoped for a better life, one free of the paternal family coalition. It had been a successful tactical operation as our extended maternal family drove us to the airport to see us off. I loosened my seat belt to peep through the Swissair plane's window and never forgot the crowd of family clapping and waving goodbye.

When Air Zimbabwe was still operational, it was standard practice to allow family members to stand or sit on nearby airport balconies facing the airports' hangers and runway. The intercom sounded, "Ladies and gentleman, we are ready for takeoff." Seat belts buckled. We were headed not just to any place in the United States but to the golden state of California. In terms of making the devil mad, how about that?

CHAPTER 9

Pharaoh's Pursuit

That flight to the United States was not my first time on a plane. We had taken occasional family vacations to Johannesburg and the beautiful island of Mauritius by plane, but that was the first time I had gone overseas.

After a stop in Vienna, Austria, Mama, Gary, baby TJ, and I experienced our port of entry into the United States via John F. Kennedy International Airport (JFK). We were jet lagged. A man helped us haul our excessive luggage to the next flight transfer lounge. It required us to exit the airport briefly. The sliding doors quickly opened, and we all suddenly were hit with humid August heat we had never experienced before. Summers in Zimbabwe were moderate with dry temperatures, so the humidity was quite a shock.

Mama was the most tired. She had had little

if any sleep as we flew because she was so worried Gary would fall into a spiritual attack. Can you imagine the panic that would have taken place in the air with Gary in a coma-like state and us not being able to explain the situation to flight attendants and nearby passengers? We were tired but so grateful to God for keeping us.

In an hour, we boarded our flight to Los Angeles International, LAX.

I woke up when the pilot announced that we were preparing to land. I looked out and saw the dazzling night lights of Southern California sparkling as far as I could see. I was so excited! We had arrived, and I could not wait to see Daddy again.

August 15, 1999, became our official family Thanksgiving Day, and we acknowledge it as an anniversary even today. I vaguely remember going through customs and immigration and wondered why we had to take our shoes off again.

We were ecstatic and dropped our bags as the sliding doors opened and Daddy's big smile welcomed us! He was so happy to see everyone. Daddy looked a bit skinnier than when I had last seen him. I suppose adjusting to the American diet and a tighter budget had caused him to drop a few pounds during the year. I thought Mama would replenish him soon with some sadza once we settled. That moment, we all felt an overwhelming sense of pure joy and freedom. We felt free to finally exhale.

Daddy drove us to our new home, an apartment in Ontario, California. He had prepared the bedrooms with basic bedding as best as possible. After our twenty-eight-plus-hour journey, we were happy to sleep on any moderately comfortable surface.

We spent the next few days overcoming our jet lag and doing some grocery shopping. I was fascinated by margarine, which tasted like cheese when spread on bread. I thought the neighborhood kids talked funny; I didn't realize that I must have sounded just as funny to them. Some of their parents looked like the wealthy Indians who ran businesses in Zimbabwe. I later learned that they were not Indians but Hispanics mostly from Mexico.

Anytime I turned on the radio, it seemed that the only thing I heard was Lou Bega's song "Mambo No. 5." No one can forget the late nineties mantra: "A little bit of Monica in my life, a little bit of Rita is all I need, a little bit of Jessica here I am, a little bit of you makes me your man!" What strange music I thought.

I joined Mama in our cozy living room most afternoons to try to watch TV. We had no cable, so we were greeted by Jerry Springer's daytime show of peculiar family conflicts, which were different from what I knew. Everyone experienced the epitome of culture shock.

A few weeks after our arrival, my parents took Gary and me to the local schools. Based on the American educational system, summer was coming to an end, and we needed to be registered and get immunization shots. Though I was looking forward to attending an American school, I realized this was not one of our family vacations. We were going to stay in the United States. *How long? When will we see our family again?* Questions rushed through my head, but I did not ask my parents for answers; I was just so happy we were all together.

The first day of school came around. I had barely slept the night before because I had been anxious about what to expect. Mama told me I didn't have to wear a uniform anymore to school, which I was surprised to hear. The American school system was entirely different from Zimbabwe's Cambridge-based curriculum. I was registered in the fourth grade, and I immediately sparked the curiosity of my classmates. "She's the new kid from Africa!" a student blurted across his group table. A girl beside me introduced herself and immediately asked, "Did you live in trees?" Another student behind me asked, "Did you have a pet lion?"

Bewildered by all their questions. I raised my hand to get the teacher's attention.

"Excuse me, teacher, may I please go to the loo?" I politely asked. The teacher looked as if he had not heard me, so I asked again, looking straight at him.

"The loo?" he asked. "Oh, you mean the restroom!" he finally said.

I shrugged. I accepted a hallway pass and made my way to the loo. *What in the world is a restroom?* I wondered. I had a lot of adjusting to do, and I sometimes laughed at some of the students' questions. The main advantage was I seemed to be doing excellent in school as I had already learned the majority of what was being taught in my new school back in Zimbabwe though I had struggled in school there.

About a month into starting school, I was finishing up my morning cereal when Mama went to check on Gary. She returned a few minutes later looking fairly distraught. I immediately had a lumpy feeling in my gut. Dreading what she may have realized, I went to Gary's room. It had started again.

I stubbornly entered his room and tried as best as I could to wake Gary up. "Gary! Gary! Wake up! You'll be late for school!" How could this be happening again? We had left Zimbabwe and had gotten away from my paternal grandmother, Uncle Jake, and other members of the coalition. Daddy was getting ready to go to his classes that morning; this was the first time he saw Gary in this condition. He had a confused look on his face; he was merely perplexed.

Due to the spiritual attacks, Gary ended up missing a lot of school. How were we to explain to the school what was going on with Gary? We were the only family we had in this foreign country. If Gary didn't go to school, my parents could get in trouble according to the law. Mama bought a phone card to call Gogo and let our extended maternal family know what was going on. We needed as much prayer as we could get. We also realized that spiritual battles were no respecter of physical location. Different continent, different time zone—but the coalition had not known we had left Zimbabwe, but Pharaoh had pursued us.

CHAPTER 10

Dinner-Table Attack

Months passed, and the battle continued. My parents resorted to having a homeschool teacher come in after hours. Daddy also managed to have him register for an adult school hosted by a nearby community college. Gary seemed to awake from his coma-like state late in the day, and that attempt at educating him would keep my parents legally compliant. Daddy tried to come up with all kinds of natural solutions to solve a spiritual problem. Could he not see the source of the problem? We had lived and survived the spiritual attacks for an entire year in his absence. Why wasn't Daddy protecting Gary and the rest of us?

Daddy was in denial. First, he gathered the family and drove us to some children's sleep center hospital. The doctors said they would monitor Gary's brain and sleep behavioral patterns overnight. It resulted in the medical experts concluding what we had already known that Daddy needed to come to terms with as well. It was ridiculous. There was nothing wrong with Gary physically, but Daddy insisted. That visit ended up costing a lot and put a strain on us financially. Next, Daddy continued with Jesus.

Daddy took us to see Jesús, someone with the Spanish name for our Lord but with an accent. It was a Saturday afternoon, and we were determined to get the help of someone who had been recommended. Daddy parked the car, and we walked into a poorly lit shop of some sort. The place smelled of incense. To my right was the register lined with decorations of grass skirts from the ceiling. To my left were all kinds of Virgin Mary ornaments, pendants, and small, medium, and large crosses. I assumed it was a store for Catholics to purchase decorative items; at least that was my educated guess. A Hispanic man greeted Daddy in an expectant manner. He was quiet and seemed to have a gentle spirit. There was something I could not quite put my finger on about him that made me nervous. *Why are we here?* The Hispanic man led us to a backroom.

"My name is Jesús," he officially introduced himself. He focused his conversation on my parents, so naturally, my eyes took in the peculiar ornaments staring down at me. I am sure if I came across the incense I smelled that day, I would recognize it.

Toward the end of our visit with Jesús, I overheard him mention to my parents something about bathing with herbs for the next week or so. Sure enough, when we got home, we all did as instructed by Jesús. I hopped in the shower, filled a bucket with hot water, and added the herbs. After cleansing my body, I obediently poured Jesús's herb-infused water all over myself. Everyone else did the same weird exercise. I think we all knew deep down that Jesús's herb-infused water would have no effect, but no one dared mention it to Daddy. Telling this story to the students at my school or the neighborhood kids would not make me the new, cool kid on the block either.

Time seemed so abstract; I had no notion of how it was going by so fast. Dealing with spiritual attacks in prayer was the norm for us. What we needed to hold onto was the power of Jesus and not Jesús's herbs.

Every night before going to bed, Mama would make sure we recited Christian prayers given to us by a pastor from Liberia who attended the same church. Sometimes, Daddy would be in his weird moods and go to the master bedroom right when we were about to pray. "I am going to bed; I am not coming there!" He would yell across the hallway. Why was he in denial? Why this strange, uncooperative mind-set? Did he not realize who the leader of the coalition fighting against us was? Daddy was with us, but he wasn't protecting us. Mama, being wise, continued to lead us in prayer with or without Daddy.

One time, TJ was watching his WWF Smackdown wrestling TV show during the evening. I had been helping Mama wipe the dishes and prepare for dinner. Mama asked me to call everyone so we could eat. Daddy was already seated at one end of the dinner table, so I called Gary. He quietly approached and leaned against the wall. Mama took the seat across from me against the wall.

Saying grace was a convenient way to get everyone seated. The aroma of freshly cooked Zimbabwean peanut butter rice and chicken stew tantalized our noses. Although the food was a minor distraction, time and time again, we desperately waited for breakthroughs. Permanent residence cards and Gary's healing were ongoing prayer topics at my family's dinner table. Praying while we waited was an emblem of hope. Youngest to oldest, everyone participated in prayers about the desolate state we were in as African immigrants.

Having just started first grade, TJ had a reasonable idea of why we kept praying. "Let us pray, God bless this food, we pray for

Gary's healing, God help us with our green card, in Jesus's name, amen." His childlike, faith-filled prayers were powerful day after day. Needless to say, his mind would then trail back to the TV for what time he could start "smelling what the Rock was cooking" for the weekly Thursday Night SmackDown wrestling show.

Then it was my turn to pray. I briefly glanced at a large watercolor portrait of three rabbits just above Mama and gently bowed my head in prayer. "Dear Lord," I started, but I was interrupted as one of the chairs made a screeching sound against the tile floor and toppled over. Gary had shoved the chair away. In a split second, He headed straight for Mama. As traumatic as it was to see my brother launching full force with his six-two stature and fist at my mother, I knew that was not Gary. A spirit had possessed him with a mission to harm Mama.

I will never forget the red eyes full of hate and evil. I instinctively grabbed TJ out of the way and shoved him behind me. When I looked back up at the chaos, I saw Daddy leaning forward to catch Gary's fist. Daddy was in between Gary and Mama. Gary's voice had changed drastically, and he shouted twice with Shona remarks coming straight from the coalition. They were full of hate and the spirit intended to cause Mama physical harm. Why?

She was our prayer warrior holding the family together by declaring the blood of Jesus over us all.

It took a few moments of Daddy shaking Gary before he came to himself. What had we all just witnessed? The coalition had sent a dinner-table attack that was beyond too far. The coalition was capable of just about anything just so my father would return to Zimbabwe. What hurt in the midst of this battle was that it had taken Daddy so much time to actually admit his mother was the culprit leading the coalition. Instead of being on the same page with his praying family, he was also experiencing the betrayal of his mother, brother, and other members of the coalition. Unfortunately, that was at the expense of Mama's pain. Mama had dealt with fighting our perpetrators without my father's full spiritual support. She had been so strong for all of us and needed Daddy's support, not denial. The dinner-table attack finally helped change that. It was time for Daddy to fight for his family with Mama.

You can imagine it was hard for me to sleep that night. Things had to change; we had to fight back spiritually: "The weapons we fight with are not the weapons of the world. On the contrary, they have divine power to demolish strongholds" (2 Corinthians 10:4 NIV).

CHAPTER 11

The Offense

A couple of days after the dinner-table attack, we were praying together. We needed to wage spiritual warfare. Gary and I had separate rooms, and Mama had asked us to switch rooms. We did, and I prayed. The next Monday morning, Gary did not wake up for school. I had extra time before walking to school because I had woken up early. I went into Gary's room and stared at him in his coma-like state. Mama was not around, but something caused me to pick up the Bible on the floor. I looked at Gary one more time and forcefully placed the Bible on his head. No one told me to do it, but somehow, I had faith in the power of God's Word. People consider the Bible's authority as the intangible power of God. My childlike faith was looking at it from a literal standpoint.

I held the Bible on Gary's head with as much pressure as I could. I was not surprised when I saw Gary's hand pop up. However, it quickly grabbed my wrist with strength like no other and certainly not expected considering his dormant state. This was not my brother. I stubbornly held on, but the spirit was digging into my wrist with Gary's nails. I let go only because I had to head to school. That incident was scary, but I walked away like it was nothing. I later told my mom about the Bible incident. Again, spiritual activities were not foreign to us. We continued to pray.

No one openly acknowledged anything, but we all knew something was shifting as we persevered in prayer. When Gary would get the spiritual attacks, he began to have visions in that state. After he would wake up, he would tell Mama what he had seen.

Sometimes after waking up from the visions, Gary would suffer from the worst migraines that even painkillers could not relieve. One of the visions I remember him telling us was how he could see ChiBagi talking. In the vision, she would be frustrated because Daddy was not going back to Zimbabwe. ChiBagi would also threaten to send more spiritual attacks on us. We would take in all the details from the visions and channel our prayers as such against her evil decrees. It was like fighting a battle but knowing what your enemy was planning before it even happened. We were on the spiritual offense.

In another vision, Gary saw himself in a container. He explained that it was as if he were miniature and had been placed in a closed peanut butter jar. It sounds outrageous, but our interpretation of the dream was that it was ChiBagi's attempt to lock Gary's destiny and intimidate us.

Other visions consisted of Gary seeing himself in third person running in Zimbabwe. In this particular vision, he had run away from what looked like ChiBagi's village hut. He said he ran away from a dark-figured man who was chasing him. When he awoke from the coma-like state, Gary said he felt as tired as if he had been physically running.

Let us ponder that last vision I just mentioned. ChiBagi had the energy, resources, connections, and time to put all this effort into what Gary described as almost spiritual teleportation. Gary essentially was in Zimbabwe while in the coma for that vision. If that effort is channeled into U.S. NASA programs, I am sure we would all be traveling and living on Mars and Jupiter by now. Or more practically, all that effort could have been spent on ChiBagi and the coalition's lives instead of focusing on us.

Regardless, God was using every arrow of spiritual attack to show Gary what was going on in the spiritual realm. Yes, the spiritual world is as real as this physical one we live in every day. We were channeling our prayers accordingly with every revelation.

I recall Gary having another vision of ChiBagi. She was threatening to do to me what she was doing to Gary. I immediately condemned ChiBagi's declaration in the name of Jesus. I looked at Gary and Mama and declared, "Never! No way!" Even though I was just ten, I knew who I was—a child of the most high God, and nothing could harm me.

Mama said, "Yes, that is good. You have to denounce their intentions so they do not materialize." Words are powerful. "The tongue has the power of life and death, and those who love it will eat its fruit" (Proverbs 18:21 NIV).

We have the authority to speak positive or negative in every situation. Thankfully as God's children, we also have the authority to condemn every evil tongue that raises itself above the knowledge of God. So when ChiBagi decided to attack me spiritually, she didn't know God had revealed it to my family and me. When God reveals something to you, it is to redeem you. I knew how to pray. Not relying on Mama's prayer alone, I prayed to God for protection and declared that no evil arrow would strike me. We were all praying as a family, together on the surprise-attack offense!

CHAPTER 12

TJ's Broken Arm

It was another week, and I headed to school as usual. I left Gary in the coma-like state in the morning. Mama was home with TJ, who was about to start preschool soon. Daddy was at work, which was more than an hour's drive away.

At the end of the school day, I calmly walked home from the bus stop. Our apartment was on the second floor, so I marched up the exterior stone steps to the door. As I walked into the apartment, Gary was moving about in the kitchen. He stopped in his tracks when he saw me and said, "Mama isn't here. She went with TJ in the ambulance to the hospital."

"The hospital!" I exclaimed.

Gary explained that TJ had been playing on the balcony and had fallen over the metal bar and onto the stone stairs. I was utterly shocked at what I heard from Gary. Daddy had been called at work and was on his way to meet Mama at the hospital. *How exactly had TJ fallen off the balcony?* The apartment balcony had railings high enough to prevent even an adult from accidentally falling over.

Mama looked so tired by the time she, Daddy, and TJ came home. It had been a long day. She sat on the couch. We all gathered to talk about what had taken place. Mama explained that she had been in the master bedroom doing a few chores and had left TJ playing in the living room. TJ, being an ordinary four-year-old, wanted to look at his bicycle that was stored on the balcony. He opened the sliding glass door himself; he had been on the balcony numerous times before on his own. There was nothing dangerous about the balcony, which overlooked the apartment playground. He was just trying to sit on his stationary bicycle and had somehow held onto the balcony metal bar and toppled over. Our downstairs neighbor found TJ crying on the stone stairs and rushed up to knock on our apartment door.

We all listened to Mama, but it still did not make any sense. That is when she mentioned that Gary had seen something. But how had Gary seen what had happened if he was still in his coma?

Perplexed, we all turned to Gary, and he

began to give us the missing details. It was true—TJ was sitting on his bicycle on the balcony. Gary said, "TJ did not fall off the balcony on his own. While I was sleeping, I saw TJ open the sliding door, but when he got on his bike, there was someone else there. It was the dark, black spiritual figure that pushed him over the balcony!"

No one asked any questions because we knew this had actually taken place. There was no way anyone would fall over the way TJ did. We immediately thanked our gracious Lord for causing him not to have injuries worse than he had. It was a miracle he had walked away from a two-story fall onto stone stairs with only a broken arm. That dark figure was sent to push TJ for something worse to happen, but God caused their intentions not to materialize.

I was not shaken. I felt rage boiling up in me toward the coalition. Sometimes in life, you go through great trials, but it gets to the point that you need to get angry and fight for your life. Certain battles take anger to push you and shift you into a deeper level of prayer. The coalition had no limits. They had gone too far, and we intensified our prayers. Mama and TJ had endured a long day. At the hospital, Mama was nervous, worried the doctors would think this might have been grounds for child negligence or something. The law in the United

States was very sensitive to those matters, but we knew she was just a concerned mother.

Once again, God had revealed to us what had taken place. My poor little brother, TJ, sat there on the sofa with his new cast on his broken arm. So with holy anger, we channeled our specific prayers that night.

CHAPTER 13

Justification

The Lord had surely been seeing my tears at night wondering when the nightmare would end. It had been fight after fight, and the battle was still going on. After another evening of family prayers, I headed to my bedroom. As I was preparing to go to bed, I stopped in my tracks.

"God, here I am. I know you are watching over us, Lord. I know everything will be all right. Father, You have protected us and even shown us so many things. I do not understand why all these attacks are happening to my family and specifically Gary. Lord, please heal my brother in Jesus's name. I just want us to live happy again and free.

"Mama went through so much in Zimbabwe when Daddy was gone. You gave her so much strength and courage. She taught us all how to pray even when Daddy was stubborn. God, please protect Mama. She does everything for us and takes care of us like superwoman. I want Mama to be happy.

"Daddy has gone through a lot too. He has changed so much since Zimbabwe and does not even drink that stinky beer anymore. Daddy prays with us and goes to church with us instead of going to play golf like he used to in Zimbabwe. We prayed that You would save him, God, and You did.

"God, please heal Gary. I plead the blood of Jesus over him. It's almost been three years, and he is still alive. Lord, You must have a purpose for his life. Let this craziness come to an end. God, protect TJ and me too. No evil spirit must come near our dwelling in Jesus's name, amen."

My family had shed a lot of tears that resulted from the challenges of being African immigrants. There were several instances when we did not know if our H-1 visas would be extended. The beautiful Greendale house had been sold because we needed the money to help cushion our shortfalls. My parents had difficulty finding jobs because they needed companies willing to sponsor them. God graciously made a way for Daddy to get an H-1B work visa. We also prayed for permanent-residency green cards though that was a long shot. These were just a few of challenges on top of the spiritual warfare we were going through. We missed our helpful maternal family. It was hard, but my parents persisted, and God helped us.

The coalition's attacks had to amount to something. I had a very real dream. I felt I was lying on my bed awake. My bedroom door was open. All the lights in the apartment were out. I felt as if someone were watching me. Sure enough, I spotted a black figure that had two solid, hollow circles for eyes and a somewhat boneless body. The dark figure was fluid, like a spirit. It leaned against the door as if peeking into my room. The figure did that twice and then disappeared the moment it knew I had seen it.

The next morning, I told Mama about this vision or dream. I was scared but knew our prayers were working. I also knew God was fighting our battle when I stopped having another vision or dream. In this one, I would be in my bedroom once again lying down face up. I would feel pressure on my feet as if someone were sitting on that end of my bed. It felt so real that I honestly was scared something else was in my room. "Lord, into Your hands I commit my spirit; into your hands I commit my spirit," I would mouth silently. Was I awake or asleep? It was real. I saw a black woman with her back turned to me sitting on my bed. But my spirit rebuked whatever was trying to intimidate me, and the pressure on my feet eventually stopped.

In the morning, we tried to wake Gary up, but he didn't. Mama decided to drag him asleep from his room and onto the living room floor. I walked away briefly. When my attention came back to the living room, Mama was standing over Gary. I looked down at Gary and was astonished at the position he was in. Still on the floor, Gary's legs were overlapped, and his arms were stretched out. His body was making a cross on our living room floor like the cross of Jesus.

What did this mean? It was a significant moment during our times in a foreign country. Deliverance was taking place daily. Every other day, Mama would let me and TJ know what had occurred when we were at school. The monitoring spirit attacked Gary when it was time to go to church, and we would often return with him still in his coma. One Sunday afternoon when we were returning from church, we entered the apartment to find that Gary had awakened earlier than usual. The shower had just stopped running, but we all could hear movements in the bathroom. Daddy opened the bathroom door to find Gary attempting to flush the toilet continuously.

"Gary, what happened? Are you okay?" Daddy inquired.

"No. I woke up and was coughing

uncontrollably. I eventually made it to the toilet and coughed out this thing I'm trying to flush." Gary pointed into the toilet bowl.

Daddy saw what appeared to be a thick, black hairball. Mama hovered around the bathroom door also taken aback as Daddy attempted to flush the unpleasant-looking thing. They eventually managed to fish it out, and Daddy took it outside. He went downstairs toward the parking lot. Near a cement wall, he prayerfully pulled out his lighter and burned the object.

What was I to make of what I had just observed? I had experienced erratic emotions and thoughts while going through these spiritual incidences. I often wondered when all the direct attacks on our family would end. *Why don't I feel normal?*

Perhaps I was worried about feeling humiliated if others learned we were the victims of a spiritual attack. What a disgrace it would be if it got out that the leader of the coalition was my father's mother, ChiBagi.

So when it came to truly opening up as a child, teenager, and even as a young adult, I hesitated. I believe it stemmed from not wanting to be found vulnerable. I was always nice, approachable, but guarded since the thought of someone mocking me because of my paternal grandmother was unbearable. It was a touchy subject for all of us especially if Daddy was present. It would have been beneficial to Mama, Gary, TJ, and me if Daddy called a family meeting to discuss ChiBagi honestly. Even one such acknowledgment would have helped us all deal with the aftermath of these attacks on the family. Living in the United States as a foreigner, I realized there weren't many people who would identify and understand what my family was going through.

Although at times I was withdrawn, I matured faster than the average girl my age. I understood spiritual warfare and the persistence it takes to be strong in the Lord. The community and even our local church may not have comprehended what was wrong, but my family and I knew the Lord was our refuge and strength. The trial was making every member of the family stronger. What you think might kill you is a tribulation in which you will experience the presence of God. If we could just hold on and be still in the storm a little longer, victory would surely be ours. We were all responsible for bringing the will of God in our lives to pass by activating the power of the word of God. Remember 1 Corinthians 15:55–58 (NIV).

> Where, O death is your victory?
> Where, O death is your sting?
> the sting of death is sin and

the power of sin is the law. But
thanks be to God! He gives us
the victory through our Lord
Jesus Christ. Therefore, my dear
brothers and sisters, stand firm.
Let nothing move you. Always
give yourselves fully to the work
of the Lord, because you know
that your labor in the Lord is not
in vain.

We were steadfast because we belonged to
Jesus Christ. Our family had no choice but to
live lives full of prayer, to be unmovable, and
to persist in prayer. Even Gary's vomiting the
hairball told us deliverance was taking place.

The spiritual trauma had been
overwhelming, but it was nothing compared
to the suffering of Jesus on the cross. It was
difficult not to begin playing the blame game
or pointing fingers about who should have
done things differently to protect the family.
We could not afford to focus on the past; we
needed to persevere in following Christ.

Sometimes, life's hardest times become
blessings because through them, we discover
God's love for us. We were thankful to God
not out of obligation; rather, we took the
opportunity to recall all the good things He
had bestowed on us. God knew what we were
going through and had never abandoned us.

Being so loving, God reminded us that we remain justified through Jesus's death and resurrection on the cross. We had hope because we had also been sanctified, set apart for God's purpose. God protected and sustained us in Zimbabwe and in the United States because He had plans for everyone in my family, including Angela, who was soon to arrive.

CHAPTER 14

The Phone Call

I had just finished fifth grade and would be going into sixth grade. Thirsty due to the hot California weather, I eagerly ran home from the bus stop for a glass of water. As soon as I was done quenching my thirst, Mama told me what had happened while I was at school.

In the morning, Daddy was headed to one of his midweek master's classes, but he was waiting around to see if he could give Gary a ride to his adult school class. Mama entered Gary's bedroom to wake him up as was her custom and boldly exclaimed, "Gary! Wake up!"

Gary slowly got up. He made his way to the bathroom, slowly showered, and got dressed. Mama returned to his room to tell him to hurry up, that Daddy was waiting to drop him off. My mama received discernment from the Holy

Spirit that she was not speaking to Gary. "Who are you?" she asked.

The spirit began to laugh rambunctiously. Mama was led to believe that it identified itself as James and was arrogantly proclaiming, "Today, we fooled you!"

The Bible instructs us to be strong and courageous; Mama prayerfully commanded James to leave at once in the name of Jesus. Every time she prayed and said Jesus, the foul spirit would shriek and beg her not to say that name. Mama went on to explain that James confessed that he and the other legion of spirits had been lied to. They had been promised to be rewarded by Gary's death, but nothing was working. God had seen all our tears and heard all our prayers the whole time; they could not touch Gary. The enemy's plans had failed; they had been defeated by the blood of Jesus.

Mama said she prayed and commanded James to leave our house with all his friends in the name of Jesus. James began walking in Gary's body throughout the apartment home from room to room. He pointed at corners and claimed his friends were hiding there. He told them to leave. James walked out of the apartment door, and Daddy cautiously followed, watching him go downstairs. Daddy held Gary's hand as Gary walked toward the street.

Mama told me, "That is when Gary tried to cross the busy street. Daddy stopped him from walking into the traffic. At that moment, we could tell Gary came to himself, and the spirit that had identified itself as James left."

"What are we doing out here, Daddy?" Gary asked in a confused manner.

From that day forward, Gary never experienced another spiritual attack. Deliverance had taken place by the blood of Jesus shed on Calvary. Gary was able to do all his work when the homeschool teacher came to check on him. He caught up in his studies at the adult school and even began playing golf for the high school team. He also took classes at a community college.

Gary knew that God had saved and healed him; he started volunteering to work the video cameras at our church. In 2004, he received the "Best Church Worker of the Year" award. We were all so proud of him. He earned several golf tournament awards as well. I had my older brother back. God had healed him, and we started doing normal, sibling activities again. Gary introduced me to basketball, and I became quite the skilled point guard practicing against six-two Gary. What he would do with his redeemed life was completely up to him. It was his journey, and we all have our own unique journey as well. In life, it is important not to judge the journey before God says it is over.

A few months later in the year, our family welcomed the new addition of Angela, my sweet younger sister. She is our angel. Her birth marked a new season in all our lives. When Angela was born, her birth was accompanied by so many other blessings. My parents continued to work diligently at multiple jobs at times. God has always been faithful in providing for us as we lived simple lives despite our overwhelming challenges. We were content with what we had because we valued life and the good health God was blessing us with every day.

Things were not easy; Daddy and Mama picked up odd jobs even on weekends. On a Saturday afternoon, one of my maternal uncles gave us the phone call. Why was it the ultimate phone call? Well, depending on your perspective, he delivered the message to Mama to tell my father that ChiBagi had passed away.

He went on to describe that in her last days, she had been having all kinds of mysterious ailments and expressing dire sorrow. I will put it bluntly—she was suffering before she passed. With all the hate you may have expected our family to show, I distinctively remember Mama praying that ChiBagi had given her life to Christ before passing away.

Mama, Gary, and I were shocked but not too sure how to respond. Daddy was still when Mama told him his mother had passed. He did not cry or fly to Zimbabwe to attend the funeral. Obviously, we all were going to take a while to get acclimated to ChiBagi's passing. She was gone along with the spirits such as James that had been attacking us. They had been defeated by Jesus, our one and only Savior.

The phone call represented the first momentous milestone in turning our wounds into scars and beginning the forgiveness process. Forgiveness is required of us as Christians not just for characters like ChiBagi but for our sake as well. We needed to forgive so we could heal and God could use our scars.

I would not trade my scars for anything. I have an obligation to show my scars and tell my story. I listened to a series once by Pastor Steven Furtick of Elevation Church. In his sermon entitled "No More Nails," he noted,

> Christianity is not cosmetic surgery, so you can hide what you have been through to try to get people to think you're perfect; Jesus Christ did not come to conceal the pain, He came to reveal His glory, and He showed it in His scars.

Here I am. We often welcome God into our presence, but God has already been here as the great I Am. We are the ones to enter His presence with all humility and acknowledge that as our heavenly Father, He has been waiting for us. He has seen every pain, wound, and tear because God has a purpose for our scars.

Let's be honest. We all have scars, dysfunctions, and we have been through struggles. Your closest friend may not know it, but God does. Let us not forget that what held us back does not hold us back anymore because of the cross. Like the ultimate sacrifice, God cannot use your wounds; he wants to use your scars. Wounds reflect life's deepest hurts, but scars reveal the healing power of God for your restoration and His glory.

What has wounded you? What trials happened or are still happening to you? Are you willing to show your scars? It takes faith to believe that the pain and wounds of the trial are healed even though you remember the hurt when you occasionally look at your scars.

God led my family and me through this testing trial to create a high level of faith in our hearts. Sometimes, God allows you to walk through your journey wondering about, questioning, and challenging your belief. If your faith is wavering, it cannot sustain the trials you need to go through in your journey of life. God allowed these spiritual attacks to happen to build our faith. As a result, today, God can use me now to inspire people and exhort them through salvation in Jesus Christ. I can encourage believers to hold onto their faith through the test. I can also admonish nonbelievers that God is real, loves them, and is waiting for them to say, "Here I am, Lord. Have your way."

This life we live is not our own. It is not about us nor will it ever be. Our lives ought to reflect Jesus in who we are. We do not have to be pastors to point people to Christ. Our best testimony is how we lead our lives. God has deposited so much in us that we have not even begun to scratch its surface.

Do you know who you are in Christ? A powerful man or woman of God wired to do what only you can do. You are the apple of God's eye created to fulfill a special assignment for His purpose. You are unique with exceptional gifts and talents and designed by God. There is no reason we should not be able to support each other. Do not compare yourself with others because you were designed by our Creator for a distinct purpose.

As you avail yourself, God will do a new thing in your life. Can you perceive it? Once you have survived a storm and painful tribulations, your journey does not end. You must tell the world what God has done for you because all the suffering is just a small part of your full story. The pain was meant to harm you, but God allowed it to happen and intends it for your good and for the saving of many lives.

Here I am.

AFTERWORD

It was a month into 2017, and like most people, I was filled with hope and excitement for the best to come. At age twenty-six, I had experienced God's goodness and faithfulness in my family, career, and education. I had acquired a Project Management Professional (PMP) certificate, and I was doing great at work and being the best example for my younger siblings I could be. Though having had blessings bestowed on me, I was not oblivious to the fact I was also undergoing a spiritual transition, one in which God had been preparing me the previous year for—a new season of my life.

I served faithfully at church to the best of my ability ushering, giving church announcements, helping youth, and whatever else I could do in God's house. Despite all those good deeds, I still had a sense of frustration; I felt there was more I could do for God. Knowing that I fell short of His glory every day, I reminded myself that the Bible tells us in Isaiah, "All of us have become like one who is unclean, and all our righteous acts are like filthy rags; we all shrivel up like a leaf, and like the wind our sins sweep us away" (Isaiah 64:6 NIV).

I prayed, *So, God, if You use us despite our filthy rags, am I doing what You need me to do right now? Am I where You need me to serve?* There was something I was supposed to be doing, and I just was not. I continued to serve and pray for God to order my steps because it was what I had been taught to do. Serving is the will of God, but what if God has a specific assignment for the season you find yourself in? Although I do not still understand everything fully, I knew my purpose was calling, and I was in transition.

To grow through my transition, God began changing so many things I was used to in my life. One of those significant changes was not only in my career but also where I would be fellowshipping. I remember vividly entering my new church for the first time during a Wednesday night Bible study. The senior pastor spoke profound words of life: "You are not here on accident and God scheduled you to be here. It is time to transition to your next level in God." I believe God leads us all to where we need to be to grow for the assignment placed on our lives no matter how much we want to stay in our comfort zones.

So on February 8, 2017, I was invited to

speak at an alumni panel at my undergraduate alma mater, George Mason University. I was enthused by the idea of encouraging business students; I answered all the challenging questions they had for me. I inspired them to know that the sky was not the limit and to continue working hard toward their aspirations.

During my drive back home, I reflected on how students had asked me what my habits of success were. I responded by attributing my success completely to God and the strength and ability He gave me to work hard. However, being honest with myself, that was not the full story. To do that, the students would need to know my background, my faith in God, the trials I prevailed over through prayer, and the family values that had formed my character. I kept on being nagged by a thought: *Write a book!*

Convinced that this was the Holy Spirit, I started talking to God in prayer as I often do while I drove. *God, how can I write a book? I do not have any experience doing anything like that. I am only twenty-six and have never been fond of creative writing. Even if I did it, what would I write about? Myself? My career? Can this be bigger than me?* These were just a few of many questions I had, but night after night, I could not sleep until I began to take the first step toward the crazy idea.

The crazy idea was a God idea. God led me

to write my childhood story and how my family and I had migrated to the United States. I had buried the memories deep in me and seldom told anyone besides one or two people, but even then, I omitted many details. All my life, I felt few could understand the turmoil and spiritual trauma I had experienced at such a tender age. But when I was twenty-six, God needed me to tell my full story and encourage them with the fact they could make it through the toughest valley with God and help others by sharing their testimonies.

Beloved God wants to use your scars; He had brought me to the point in my life that I was healed and ready to finally share my story. But you can do God's assignment only His way, so I prayed, worshiped, and meditated on the story of Joseph in Genesis.

Through the inspiration of the Holy Spirit, I began writing on Thursday, March 2, 2017, and completed my first draft by Wednesday, March 8. Yes, this book was written in a week. I was speechless at what had transpired and just praised God. I had no experience writing; all I had was a willingness to learn and allow God to use me.

Still in March, God—the master orchestrator—sent the right people into my life to help me bring this assignment to pass. On Wednesday, March 15, I spoke with a publishing specialist working for WestBow Press, a subsidiary of

Thomas Nelson & Zondervan. This is one of the major Christian publishers that also produce the New International Version Bibles.

In deep focus, I told no one except my mother what I was working on. For many years, I had encouraged her to write a book on what our family had gone through. However, she was still working her way through the phases of forgiveness. But after she witnessed me in my season of transition, I knew I would also help her with her message when the time was right.

I would never have imagined anyone telling me on New Year's Day in 2017 that I would become an author. But here I am, learning every day to trust God on this journey of life.

Do not focus on your shortfalls; just make yourself available for God's agenda. It really is not about you. Yes, people you used to associate with may even get upset because they do not understand the sudden change in you. Others may question why you are no longer doing what they are used to seeing you do. The craziest ideas are often God ideas if you cross-check them with the Bible. God speaks to everyone through His Holy Spirit, His Word, and even other people.

In the midst of your hectic life, stop and listen. Draw closer to God, and keep listening to what He needs you to do in the season you are in by just saying, "Lord, Here I am. Have your way in my life."

CPSIA information can be obtained
at www.ICGtesting.com
Printed in the USA
BVOW03s2028110817
491884BV00001B/3/P